Decade
The First Ten Years

Christopher Lewis

PublishAmerica
Baltimore

© 2005 by Christopher Lewis.
All rights reserved. No part of this book may be reproduced, stored in a retrieval system or transmitted in any form or by any means without the prior written permission of the publishers, except by a reviewer who may quote brief passages in a review to be printed in a newspaper, magazine or journal.

First printing

At the specific preference of the author, PublishAmerica allowed this work to remain exactly as the author intended, verbatim, without editorial input.

ISBN: 1-4241-0485-8
PUBLISHED BY PUBLISHAMERICA, LLLP
www.publishamerica.com
Baltimore

Printed in the United States of America

Penobscot Violin

The porch flares out past the front door,
Tin roofs drip rain into the grass,
Leaves won't blow away with the wind,
The streets are empty.

Small towns are that way sometimes...
Lazy on Sunday afternoons
After everyone's home from church,
The dinner's all been eaten.
It seems, sometimes,
That even time stops

On Sunday for a nap.

Every now and then, though,
If the weather's just so
And the lemonade's been sweetened
Enough to make your tongue wiggle,
Mr. Ames will open his window
And let the breeze pass through.

He takes it out of the case
And begins to play a tune.
And it's the sweetest tune anyone's ever heard.
Plays...
It matches the Sunday, though;
Rather brings out the laziness—
The kind of music you play just before a nap.

Well, that's how small towns go.

Mr. Ames' has been gone seven years.
But every now and then,
On a Sunday,
If the weather's good,
The lemonade's been sweetened,
And even though the wind's blowing,
The leaves are still,
Mr. Ames plays his violin.

American Gothic City Blues

I like the color green sometimes,
But sometimes isn't always enough.
Like wet crackers on Thursday morning,
She's rustling newspapers in the corner
And the bugs run away when the lights come on.
Cold air and snow pour through the cracks,
And bookkeeper wins 'cause it's the only one with three
    pairs of letters.
We mustn't forget about the four-letter words-
He watches her in the library bathroom—
The lights flicker and fade.
He can't finish writing the curse words on the wall.
Maybe he can't spell correctly.

American Gothic City Blues II

A crack in the counter's dingy surface—
She calls her friend from a payphone downstairs,
Her baby screams, wails for hunger.
The electricity's off…bill's overdue.

Many walls to climb, many sights to see,
If only she had the time.
Money might be nice,
But then again…

The payphone rings again,
But it isn't for her…
Boss gave her the last check today.

XMAS

Blood soaked ashes
Rain into my hair.
Clothes,
Stained with smoke.
The streetlights
Flicker in/out of sync.

The sign says "MERRY CHRISTMAS"
And the last bulb
On the "S" is burnt.
Voices carry
From the streets above.

Rusty grating
Leaks the stale water
Onto my swollen head.
Like battery acid,
It eats at me.

My small world's seclusion;
Solitude…

A party going on around me,
But I want to mingle with no one.
The world spins by me,
And I stop to watch it pass me by.

The fresh ink pours out
As I wash my notes away from the page,
The old jumbles of rhythms beat
The back of my head.

Westbank Expressway

We passed through
Crescent City
On our way somewhere.
We drove along the Westbank.

Ramshackle shotgun houses.
The kind of neighborhoods trying hard
To fight against extinction's horizon.

The expressway, like a snake,
Curving in and out of homes and
Buildings and
Yards and parking lots.
Constricts like a boa.

Why?

A man carries a gun into a store.
Shoots clerk, takes cash, runs away.

A policeman seals off the scene, takes evidence
And goes on home. Eats a doughnut, unaffected.

A small child eats nothing. Mother's gone—
Don't know where. Ain't ever coming home.

The blood from her wrists,
The cracks in the pavement,
The clouds, freed from the heavens,
Rain hatred down on salvation.
The carpet burn on her legs
Can't have hurt as much
As the cut on her neck.

Movie star eyes
Razor blade scars.
Full red lips
Rope burns on her neck.
Breathy sighs.
Track marks on her arms.
Voluptuous hips
Bruises on her cheeks.

Death pours from her eyes
Tears still forming from her long, painful cries.
Hateful rain falls on our faces;
Flashbulb lights fill the place. A morbid effect,
Like tales of neglect.

Cyberfukt

Hi def, Web TV, computers and modems.
Encyclopedias on CD-ROM,
And entire libraries in a ten diskette box.

We wear the names of
Our favorite players,
Our favorite fashion moguls,
Our favorite Cuban Nationalists.
Heads swarm with ideas
Of revolution, of evolution,
And of fashion
All at the same time.
Our cars get faster;
Our minds get slower.

Materialism, apathy, and trivial knowledge
Overlap a weak sense of culture
And a defined lack of intelligence.
How can we be the hope for the future
If we have no hope for ourselves?

Designer fashions = free advertisement.
Book deals and TV rights for murderers and rapists,
Everyone wants to be connected.
Designer drugs mixed with Old World nostalgia,
All tied together with a TV News special.
Justice on the television and radio.
A jury of twelve

Million peers.
The world's in a heightened ignorant state.
"Today's top story: A turkey dies in Peru!"

Perchville

Evening.
Perchville Road.
Two of us
Swung our feet
Off the bridge.

I watched our feet swing.
Concentrated.
The way our laces
Barely tipped that water.
They made delicate waves
That rippled out.
I loved the way our waves meshed.

Her words, my words—
Nothing but a rhythmical hum,
But at the time, it didn't matter.

Capricorn

Wow...
Such a different dream.
The stars give
A command performance—
Dancing, jumping, acting
Just for us.

I turn to the side,
See you lying next to me.
Our eyes connect,
And I am drowning.

As you see me,
I wonder what you see
Buried deep in my eyes.
As we interlock,
The world is in total harmony
And you and I
Are at the helm.

Trust me,
Because I don't
Believe In anything
Because I won't.

She thinks of things we can't remember,
And talked of games we never said
We'd even consider playing.

But I was ten and she was twelve,
And that was the summer of love
For me, but it wasn't '67.

I enjoyed her presence, every second,
And called her when we were apart
For longer than even ten minutes.

She asked me one day if I knew
All the pretty things we could see
In an ink blot if we really looked.

Always Maybe

Almost always
Sometimes
I find
Myself lost
In those eyes,
And I stare
In wild amazement
About these weird
Feelings of elatement
And I am wanting
To be sedated.
Yet, life works
So mysteriously
And love,
More viciously
Than a tiger's strike.
It attacks from behind
And leaves me blind
Like from The new winter's snow.

I sang my song
Of sad depression,
And held up my hopes
For this obsession,
But found a hole
And fell in it.
I could climb out
But I didn't.
I hurt my head on certain thoughts
And broke my nerves on my distraught

Attitudes.

It seems I've been this way forever.
But life, it seems,
Tires to be clever
In its evil ways And sadistic plays
On a tired mind.
She's so close to me in such a way,
But stands at such a sad distance away,
And I am so blackened
That I can't grasp.
The pain is so fierce
And it strikes like an asp.

What a disappointment
It is to be this way
Each and every day.
But it's a sadness I can find
And be alone with my own kind
And destroy my mind.

But it's always a pleasure.
It's my only constant,
My only treasure.

Hey, it only lasts a lifetime…

Once, in the Time of Fairies

Can you remember the time of fairies?
A time of bold comparisons
To the totally dead world around us?
That time I dreamt of something beautiful?

Can love ever be achieved?
No one can imagine the pain—
My twisted metal spine,
The fluid around my brain—
Sorrow.

Shine

Tomorrow morning
Breaks through, and
The sunlight Catches a glimmer
In her crying eyes.
She wakes
Up next to her demons
And asks herself
What happened
To her angels
That were there the night before.
Things just about couldn't get any worse,
Then memories came,
Fading back too fast,
And the night before
Sends her back
To the birthday of a ghost.

Am I Wrong?

I felt death again today,
Sorrow won't go away.
I try to scare it away, I'm screaming,
But it always comes back when I'm dreaming.
It brings fear along, they taunt me.
I try to run, but they follow to haunt me.

With fear comes death,
Then the epiphany of solitary.
A quiet repose at the gate of a mortuary.
But the agony of being alone
Hurts so much that I can't be strong.
All you can say is that I am wrong?

The Death of Nowhere Anymore

Got a pocketful of death
To go along with all my wealth.
Bluesin' with a rattlesnake
Trying to forget about a heartache,
Chopping down old oak trees
With razor-bladed memories.
Frowning on the indecency
Of daylight's obscenity;
It's wicked mutilations,
Designs of false creations.

I daydream myself to far away;
To a distant, but familiar place
That is guarded by an angry sun
That doesn't shine on anyone.
It just eats away at my remains,
Slowly driving me insane.

Times Like No Other

And it's the good things
That roll around naked at your feet.
And it's the great things
That parade around senseless in the streets.
No one knew exactly what
Was happening to them.
They all knew exactly what
Was happening to him.

We sat quiet in the corner
Singing songs about our mothers,
Playing games for the summer—
These were times like no other.

He played guitar
In the French Quarter at noon.
We wrote some songs
And sang them at the moon.

We walked away from trouble last night.
We felt like getting in a bar fight.
So, we packed it up, and took it to the streets
With nothing but our songs and our old blue jeans,
The beer cans stacked up in the barn,
And my drunk ass passed out on the lawn.

Animosity

How dare you raise your hand to me?
You are not my keeper!
You are not my equal!

White

What's with you guys?
Not enough needles, pills, electricity?
What else can you take from me?
You dissect my life for study.

The 7th Level

The fundamentals of such,
Being imperfect.

Dealing with devils,
Comfort in being alone.

Too many times,
Inconsistencies?

A catalog of fame
And fortune hidden away.

Many more dealings
With unnatural things.

We mass-produce
The perfect mind.

I can't do anything with myself anymore,

Seasons

Toilet water genius with an infinite perception;
Such a glutton for punishment.
A plastic little Jesus—Immaculate Conception;
A valid source of malnourishment.
Tiny capfuls of poison infiltrate my head.
Every change of season makes me wish I were dead,

Conviction.
Can you say it with a straight face?
Addiction.
Can you keep up with the pace?
We pretend that it does not hurt;
We play make-believe.
Condescend. Doomed from birth
To live a life of grief.

Everything for One

Broken lights, scattered along the sidewalk

Faint, lingering perfume, wispy.
Smoke…

I can hear it…
Heels, clicking on the pavement
Running through the glass.
Heads turned.

Neon blue, red, and green
Flicker on and off, casting rainbow shadows
Against my face.
I see it in the window's reflection.
She's running from me?
Gunpowder scent overcomes
    Tangy blue—
All quiet after thunder?
Calm before the storm.

Was I running from her?

Funny—

Try to think of something funny.
Like someone looking over my shoulder while I write this,
Snickering quietly to myself.
The person about which I am writing
Is the same person standing over my shoulder reading.

Try to think of something funny.
Like knowing beyond all doubt that the little men in the
 traffic lights
That change the signals from green to yellow as I approach
Are the same little men that live in the car stereo,
And turn on my favorite song, just as I reach my
 destination.

I find myself staring at her.
I can see through her inhibitions
Into her warm moistness…
I imagined myself slipping in and out of her illusions

Wind blew across her face as her lips neared mine.
The air, tinted with fresh rain and her sweet breath,
Tickled my nose as I inhaled everything she gave me.

REMEMBER

I saw your smile in a photograph,
And I thought to myself.
I had to laugh about how long it's been
Since I've seen you last.
How long has it been since we've kissed?
I can't remember, but I know it's something that I missed,
Along with all the other things I wish I had the nerve to list.

I heard your voice from the razor blade.
I cried into the bed we made.
I wondered why I let you go.
Thought, "why'd you go where I could not follow?"
I want so badly to be with you, to hear your voice, to come to you.

All I want is one more chance to say I love you.

5

I'm reminded as I drive northbound along the 5
Of the flag overhead, flying.
Watching all the cars driving,
Seeing the head and tail lights
Flowing, like the bars of red and white,
Speak of something more majestic
Than merely automobiles, new or classic.

On the Beach

Her hair,
Bathed in salty sunlight,
Dripping with the clean,
Sandy smell of the ocean.

My mouth,
Filled with nothings and nonsense,
Dribbling about the weather,
Warm and windy ocean breeze.

Her eyes,
Blazing white hot blue,
Filled with whimsical reflections
Of clouds and other commotions dancing.

My head,
Filled with lucid lies
About what I did
To take her away from it all—

Why I am here…

I love her like fire,
Bare-knuckled,
White with desire.

I pale in her presence
And squint
Because I'm blind from her essence.

I weaken
When I see her
Even though my strength seems to deepen.

If only I could say to you all the things I want from you…
Pains in me can only be quieted by you…
Save me from my madness and hold me to your bosom
While I pray that everything will work out in the end.
I didn't want to hurt you, I wanted to hold you,
And pretend that you hold me.
As we embraced, I couldn't help but recognize
All the hateful things you said about me
As I walked behind you…
All I want is to love you,
All you want is to find a way to hate me…

All I dream of is you,
Even as I lie in wait.
The only person to ever challenge me
And make me feel alive.
I will never dream again, unless you walk among them.
Here, I wait for you again, dwelling on what could never be,
And these stone walls remind me
That all I wanted was to love you,
And all you wanted was to kill me.

Sleeping

Boots on, but unlaced.
Blue jeans, belt undone.
Head cocked slightly to the side,
Eyes closed.
We just had a conversation,
But she couldn't manage to finish.

Overstuffed black sofa,
Cold, yet inviting, like the night.
She sinks in toward the bottom.
It swallows her, engulfs her, envelopes her,

The struggle is there,
Though not a hard fight.
The darkness gets the best of her.

So peaceful,
I watch her.

Quittin' Time.

It's five o'clock on Tuesday
And I am not all right.
Once again, I stayed
Way too late last night,
Trying not to reacquaint
Myself with all those songs we'd sung
So long ago when we were young.

But beauty has relationships with pain.
Now all I can do is pray for rain
And curse the warmth that never came
To wash me to the same place I hoped you'd be waiting.

Savior

It's a cold place,
Lonely and dark, away
From your scent,
Essence…sweetness.

    Tears roll down along
    The chasms in my face,
    Signs of weathered, beaten.

Older now, but feel the same
As a young teenager during the climax.,
Unrequited lovers?

    I ask your favor,
    Grant me please,
    One more taste,
    One more vision,
    One more lie,

It's the last, I swear!

A Mighty River

Why can't I think of anything else?
My river swells…breaks through the levee.
Mind wanders far from this place,
Then comes crashing back,
Waves full of angst and hate.

Broken bottles, lovely virtue
Spilled along the cracks in the pavement.
They run out along the quickest route away.
Like a river, they follow the path
I can't speak.
The water (love) chokes my throat,
Grasps my breath.

I drowned,
The sour droplets
Meander down against my face,
I lie slack, molded to the pavement,
Eyes fixed, staring…dreaming…praying.
HELP!
No one hears,
I can't hear myself
My thoughts so loud,
Pounding rhythm.
Blackness closing…
She left me   alone
          Again.

The Secretaries' Window

What does the eye allow us to see?
    The secretaries' window------
Drapes pulled.

    Strong silhouettes cast on the floor,
Tinted.

Rays flood in through cracks in the drapes
Illuminating dust,

    Quiet.

    Sun reflects off her curves
    The blood in her hair------
    Golden skin.

Blood on the carpet,
No breath.

Light Bulb

Swings…
Exposed wire, chewed and eroding
Metal pull chain hanging----
Swings as first been pulled.

Blackened bulb----
    Once illuminated concrete walls,
    Sunken floors,
    Stained from
    Grease and urine…

Now,
Blackness.

Dance with new magic,
See with new eyes.
Like nowhere I've ever been...
Tomorrow,
The skies roll blue again.
Sunday,
    The new smiles have come...
    Teeth, truth, blazing
    White as heat.

What's on your mind?
I turned my hand from my love.
The last time
She read from her, I cried.
Lasting in a moment.
"It's on my mind again,"
She said,
"I can't let you in."
It's all my time again.
I said, "I can never be like him."

What's on your mind?
I run my hand across the fire in her eyes.
This time, I died
Forever in a moment
The last time.

"It's on my mind again,"
She said,
"Won't you come in?"
It's all my time again.
I said,
"I will never be like him."

So worthless, yet
He's so perfect.
I'm worthless, and
I'm not perfect.

To Disappoint...

I said, "please come over."
You said, "I'll try."
You said, "I love you."
I said, "why?"
He said, "I hate you!"
I said, "it's about time!"

Geometry

I drove parallel to a train
    And stood perpendicular to rain
    As it established itself against my skin
    And collected in a puddle in my hand.

    To ponder the longitude of trains,
    To taste the freshness of the rain,
    Or bask in the glow of colored light
Is praying to god that she made her flight.

Diving to the Misanthrope

Got the inside track on divinity,
Slightly jaded with obscenity,
Riddled with silly amenities.

A small crisis of identity;
Harboring hateful pity
Slipping through the spin of society.

I've left me with quiet clarity—
No far cry from utter frailty,
Just enough to hinder ability.

Stand aside for the ministry;
Open the door to obscurity—
Fire my weapons toward destiny!

Another Interesting Decision

I guess this is kind of like strangers,
Together like this, despite any dangers
That may come from two people like us
Knowing each other as such.

It seems I've spent these last nights crying,
Wondering why I've given in to all the lying
I've been hearing from you about the picture
Of us and all those promises about the future.

I am feeling the strain of missing us
And I am beginning to lose the will to trust.

What a battle we chose to fight—
One that keeps us apart every night.
I'm battling my wits for just the slightest insight
About whether or not this is right.

Passionate

I guess this is, by chance, my passionate beginning.
Long may I run in those glistening meadows.
The delicate destructions due to sunshine's glory,
Opening several eyes as I ascend.

We begin to notice our quiet instabilities
Right as we adjust to the ever-lightening morning,
And as the sleep breaks free from around our eyes,
Hues of inconsistencies sparkle around that dazzling openness.

In this particular moment, this instant of infinity,
We should recognize that, for the last time this day
This openness is here, with the ability to renew
The instant is infinite—

This is my passionate beginning.

How Desire Begins...

I still see the soulful expression on your face,
Like memories of my favorite days
Have just seemed to be all wiped away.
I can't understand why
It hurts me so much to see a single tear in your eye,
But I know that being here is reason enough for sadness.
On the other hand, I know to leave would be madness.
The inscriptions left on the tablets of time
Point to this at the start of a line
Drawn in the sand
With the swollen finger from the broken hand
Of the god of all that was never mine
In the first place.

We began with a simple understanding,
Just a place to vent our hopeless meanderings,
And it evolved into a place with more than a lifetime's worth of illusions.
How unfair to base a love so pure, so simple, so honest on one small piece of confusion.
Moreover, how did we manage to accept nothing less
Than the slow, painful poison that this might never rest.

Sidelines

So here we stand with our backs against the wall
I remember when we could stand so tall.
Now, nothing but a memory,
The times we shared, you and me.
I tried everything, you know,
Just to get to you, but I guess you had to go
And now I am always going to be without
The love of my life.
I doubt I will ever understand what it means
To watch from the sidelines
While everyone finds happiness for lifetimes.

A long time ago,
I began this journey with a belief.
Maybe it's just me,
But now that I am older, I am beginning to see
That things are never so definitive or equal
As when I say, "I used to be beautiful."

To Share Orion's Belt

She asked the way to Orion's belt.
I told her exactly how I felt.
I left her the night after
Because of several small disasters.
Now I am no good again.
I drove myself home in the rain.
The sun decided to come out today
Trying to dry the water filling my brain.
But as the story goes, time after time,
The same old shit, the same old rhymes.
Here we go again on the broken carousel
Dreaming, "if only things had gone well."
Maybe this is the end, or another beginning.
Maybe it's my heart, telling me logic is winning.
All I know, though, is what I see,
And it's your future, lover, without me.

I Want to Be

I want to live like a hurricane,
So fast, so strong
And at the center of everything.

I want to be just like you.
I want to know
What it takes to drive you.

Into my arms, or maybe
A bit further
A little past sanity.

I want to live like a wet dream,
Everything so perfect,
Like you need me to be.

I just want to be
Part of you,
Not just a simple fantasy.

I need to be
Inside me
So I can save me.

All Saint's Day

As I genuflect to pray this morning,
Forgetting that its god that I'm ignoring,
I couldn't seem to remember
Everything I needed to get it together.

My smile is broken and glaring,
Stained from all the cigarettes I'm inhaling
While I ponder what it is I'm actually doing
Going around in circles, forgetting what I'm pursuing.

And it's been a long time coming, I guess,
Wondering if I'll carry through this mess.
It's all I can do to find a breath of faith
Enough to keep the devils inside for the Feast of All Saints

He brought up an interesting point to me today,
Something about life's duality.
It definitely gives me something to think about.
It's been a colorful day to say the least.
Not a chance goes by that I don't retreat
To the sanctum of everlasting doubt.

To pierce the night like shadows in the rain;
To truly understand the brotherhood of fame,
One must enter a room with no way out.
How intimidating it must be to comprehend
What it feels like to lose a friend
Or know what it means to go without.

We Should

And Saturday morning's just a memory now.
Watching cartoons, bowls of sugary cereal, and how
We used to soak up every vitamin we could
From the sunshine beaming through the neighborhood.
Now, its in a place called, "we should."

    We should get together, I haven't seen you
    In a while. We should have coffee, renew
    Those old bonds of friendship, so worn.
    I haven't seen you since before my daughter was born.

Alas,
Some things, I know, are better left in the past,
But I can't help but wonder how different
Or interesting things would be had we spent
These last years in contact.
Maybe just a phone call or a post card.
Sometimes Saturdays hit pretty hard.

I remember your last words
Like they were the ending of eternity.
You said you couldn't make it now,
But that you wanted to be with me.

Now, its years later,
But time seems to have been standing still
And I know it should be better now,
But its not, and I guess it never will.

Not Exactly.

I find it interesting that I can't lay my hands on exact;
To always wonder if everything's in tact.
This slow time's gotten stale…expired.
It feels like everything's on fire
And I can not escape its path.

It's so hard to continue looking around
When I can't get my feet off the ground.
Certain miniscule deviations
Call for complete redecoration.

"My sentiments exactly," she questioned
Without the slightest hesitation.

New Smyrna

I thought I'd never see the sunrise
As glorious as the vastness of oceans in your eyes.
And all that's left to be discovered;
It's just a dream of truths left uncovered.
And all those oceans run so deep,
But never reach far enough
To wash away those demons that I keep.
It's been a long day here, sitting in the sand,
Staring endlessly at the imprint you left with your hand.
It was all I could do not to cry
When the last memory I had of you
Got washed away with the tide.

Mosaic

All at once, the fleeting images I have
Return, but only for a glance
At a simpler time, a simpler life.
They all compile into a lie
As intricate and as disastrous to me
As the moment you first saw through me.
I find myself alone against the morning sun,
Crippled by the distances I've run
In an effort to get away
From those shining, blinding rays
That sparkle on the oceans turning black
To blue, reminding me that I'll never go back
To you. It's an ever-darkening mosaic pattern.
I've tossed in a pebble just to watch it scatter.

I can't keep up with the sunlight
No matter how diligently I try.
I run so hard, lose my breath, my eyes water over.
All I can do is a pray for a little cloud cover.

Last Walk
It was several years ago…
(I've got fifteen miles to go)
This conversation's gotten old.
It's been fifteen minutes or more
Or less than that, I don't know.

It seems I still can't let go
(Could have been fifteen years ago)
I tried to find all the time I've sold.
Now suddenly it's growing cold.
What can I do to save my soul?

It was several hours ago.
You're beautiful, please don't go.
If you do, please take my soul
Because I don't need it anymore.
I've only got fifteen steps to go.

Something about the fires
At the tops of refineries

At that point—

None of us are liars
Or bigots, or minorities,
Just lovers, one in the same
Dreaming of a simple lick of the flame,

At that point…

We see who we all are
Orange hue is the color of truth

At that point—

Relief can't go too far
And faith is never wasted on youth.

Everything is so crystal clear
And everyone I love is standing here.

Chances Are

It began with nothing more than a glance,
But in reflection, I saw a chance,
An entire gallery of imagery in an instant.
Everything I've ever wanted in a memory, so reminiscent.

Or it very possibly could have been a wink,
Some sort of innuendo, only to make me think
About what I could do to earn those thoughts
And looks, whatever I need to show I've fought for you.

She Was So Nervous

You couldn't see the elegance in her hand because she shook.
She kept her wall solid by never letting go of her book.
She bounced her eyes off anything that could cause something of a reaction
Or better yet, develop into a distraction.
I tried to show her its ok to hold my hand—
Not necessary to put up such a stand.
All I want is to gain your trust,
But it's difficult because you're so nervous.

Sunshine's Honor

An empty page or a solid white canvas—
Opportunity before me, yet my chances
Seem so slim, and yet, so dangerous.

Feels like I've stared at the sun's glare in the mirror
For hours, but nothing about myself is clearer,
Just a simpler understanding of the things that anger us

Every time I try to walk, I fall.
Exit sign's painted over the brick wall.

The doorway to eternity doesn't open for me;
I'm left alone to wander through obscurity.
And sunrise always gets the best of me.

Dark circles under my eyes, I haven't slept in days.
I'm afraid of the familiar and it's darkened place
Because it reminds me of my own face.

Now I'm stuck here in the sky
Watching sunrise through your eyes
Because I can't use mine to see
Cause sunrise gets the best of me.

Certain Recognizable Smells

It began as simply as anything else,
The same sights, the same familiar smells,
The same everything led me to believe
This was a goal I'd never achieve.
Quickly though, I saw how much more complicated
This really was, and how grossly underrated
I'd left thinking this was.

And just then I realized how much
I longed to simply feel your touch
Or my fingers through your hair.
So I shied away; though it was better than to stare
But all I wanted was to embrace you
And whisper lovingly as I face you
That this is everything I hoped it was.

I hope this night lasts forever.

An Ode to Her...

Every now and then
Rain drops on her forehead—
She gasps again when
The wind blows through her hair.
And the quiet, subtle romance
Like leaving footprints in the grass.
Those comfortable nightmares
Remind us that nuances
Can almost never last.

And it makes me smile sometimes to know
The essence of a world is in its shadow
And that life, like the beginning of a shower
Can sometimes start at fifty miles an hour.

A cross-country car ride
Make use of the instance it provides.

Hang Glidin'

Lately, I've been able to see myself from the air;
Lofty, gliding overhead while I'm just standing there
Doing what I normally do, saying what I normally say
And just not letting anything get in the way.

I love the feel of air under my feet…
Much more calming than concrete.
Or should I say more flexible than cement.
In terms of how little I have lent
Myself to better intentions, or even
Growing closer to something I believe in.

But sadness has its virtues, and youth
Has its never-ending search for basic truth;
However, when everything that's left to be said is
I prefer to know where my head is.

What Do You Want From Me?

What about me do you find so appealing
That you feel the need to keep me reeling,
Struggling with that certain absence of foresight
To understand that something about us just isn't right.

Everything about this comes dangerously close to
Being some deviant host to
Some masochistic ritual.
We only allow it because it's habitual.

How startling and frightening it is to recognize
That though I love you, I am ostracized
For only wanting what is best for both of us.
I never cared about what anyone thought about the growth of us.

But now it seems to make more sense to me
What everyone is saying about the way it should be
And how I realize that this is all wrong
And I should have seen it all along.

But hindsight is always filled with clarity
And, though it's far too late to change this tragedy,
Maybe someone will learn from me,
And that is to never be too needy.

Evenings at the Fireside

The story of my life opens wide
Kind of like the changing of the tides.
It approaches the subconscious
Like unnamed heroes that walk amongst us.
Now, all that's left is bitterness
And though I couldn't be more generous,
That life has left nothing for togetherness.

We laid out underneath the stars,
Staring up to the sky from the hoods of our cars.
The universe, broken open from inside,
Looks like spilled paints across the sky.
But it's that very same openness that I crave
Like the salt washing over me from waves.
I discovered my life(love) through it, seeming
That every little thing or event has meaning.

But because of different hearts and minds
Contradicting like lights on shadows and time,
I know the answer's just not as clear
As it used to be, and now another year
Left for the record, for posterity.
Yet, we still don't approach with any more clarity.

Even though I know I can't sing,
I still can make it interesting.
I hope I have something worth listening to,
So I'll try my best to start at the beginning.

And when the atomic clock finally stops ticking

And the Liberty Bell stops ringing,
The one thing that we can learn from this
Is that its always so hard to just exist.

Missing?

Why does it always seem like something's missing from my life?
Is it simply because I no longer have a wife?
Do I desire to be one of those thirty-year-old club dwellers
Who still cook in restaurants and live in cellars?
What about the old guys that hang out with the college kids,
Only to be left out of all their special events?
Does this come close to desirable?
Or is this just part of me being questionable?

Or is there really anything missing?
Could I simply be reminiscing?
Does it necessarily mean that I have regrets,
Or is it just that I haven't finished growing up yet?
Which, in turn, begs the question
That am I really ready for this transition
Of being once a child, now a man... Or even if it is as simple a plan
As me just going through life with the same feelings
As everyone else who gets to this point and finds himself still needing.

> Is it foolish of me to always question why
> Things have gone the way they have, possibly
> Even to wonder if I could take it all back,
> But the world is an ever-changing place,
> And though I may be flat on my face,
> I could never be too far to be off track.

It has only entered my mind lately
Since I've seen all my peers be flaky
And take on all the traits of old fashioned adults
While I still cling to the fact that I'm not yet at fault

For not finishing my journey down this highway,
Or not coming to terms for doing it "my way"
But maybe, just maybe, I think that no matter what anyone might say,
The way that I have chosen might in fact be the right way.

It is so simple to me
That everyone should see
The person that I have grown to be
Is the shell that's right for me.
And that's no one's business,
Or at least it shouldn't be,
What I choose to do with me
Or my life as I see
It as part of this dimension's reality.

I love that I am so indecisive,
And relish the joy that my life is,
And I treasure each of my friendships,
And want nothing more of any of it
Unless I can keep what I've already bought from it
So, have I figured out what's missing?
Sure, I have and its not that I'm reminiscing
Or really spending too much time wishing
That I really was somewhere else living…
The only thing I'm missing…

is nothing.

Dali Church

I drove down the highway going west
And crossed something that caught my interest.
I saw what seemed to be a cathedral
Or church or chapel, yet it was so surreal.
I guess because the angles weren't quite straight
Or maybe because it needed a fresh coat of paint.
The roof was slung on, kind of,
And it was tin, like the kind I'm fond of,
But it still didn't seem to fit.
I've never seen another one like it.
Yet, that still doesn't explain
Why I look at this with a certain
Disturbance, like something not sitting well.
It had something I've always felt
Goes against the idea of religion.
Now, I recognize the blur in my vision—
It had to do with an ornament…
The church had an M1A1 tank in front of it.

Lately...

Lately, I've treated every single memory
Like it was my worst enemy.
I can't seem to muster the courage
To allow myself the ability to flourish
Or sit against the setting evening sun
And not hate that you were the one
Who broke all my walls down.

Now all my memories are ghosts
Of all the things I've hated the most
And all the things I've ever loved can't be turned to gold
Midas will be the daydream when I can't take the cold.
Love comes when scheduled early
Is only an excuse for you not to hurt me
Or ever come when I'm not around.

Untitled

Building castles in the sand
Holding eternity in my had
A drop of rain lands on your cheek
I kiss your face to wipe it clean.
Picasso's nude is on my wall
I stare at it, hoping you would call.
Wasting another day on the sofa
But everything just takes getting over.
The rhythm of piano interludes
Makes the curves along your attitude change moods
And desire reinvents itself again.
You shift to understand the groove that we are in.
I stand out on the balcony to
Wrap my arms around your memory.
In my fifth floor lakeside apartment
Your whisper lingers here like fulfillment.
Now we're driving along the highway going west.
Shifting gears, skipping years away from the past,
I hold your hand to quiet my nervousness
And squeeze your hand to tell you I said yes.

What it Really Means to be a Raindrop.

The porch swing creaks every time it moves.
I hear the rain hit tin as it drops on the roof.
Today is a day that reminds us all that
We should take a little time to realize what's happening.

The same weekend, but the rain has subsided.
Everyone in his own space, the house is divided.
Not by anything else but a slight difference of opinion
About what to do with the rest of the evening.

Sometimes I pray for the rain to come back
So we can, all together dream of the crack
In the sky where the sun shines through after raining
And beams a ray of warmth to all those complaining.

Drops like this remind me of how simple it could be
If we all chose to not be so complicating.
All that life is, is a series of rainstorms
That makes you stop in between them to enjoy the warmth.

Highway Song

When I look at you, I'm on my knees.
Everything smells like it used to be.
I'm back, but nothing's new to me.
It's the same scars, the same enemies.

I can't shake this constant fear
That I don't know what I'm doing here.
Everything I own is borrowed
Just need a little time—hold off on tomorrow,

Your standard is so high I just can't reach
Even though the bar is at my feet.
It works like everything else;
They take until there's nothing left.

Write my rhyme to the highway song
The same sad tune's been around so long
Everyone knows how the old song goes.

Everything I know
Fits into a snapshot.
I remember it was the last spot
I stood in to see you leave.

Nothing I show
Fits anything a whole lot,
But I can see it as if it were still hot
Off your lips like you just said it.

I crave your love,
I want you wrapped in my soul.
I need to feel you shine
Like a light brightening my black hole.

I miss your touch
Like needles miss the stick;
The cold truth of the vein, so much
The harshness of the cold.
You are everything I need to know.

Protect(her)

When she's with me
I must protect her.
Alone—
She'll never know the fear
From which I suffer.
It's a little
More difficult than solitude,
Kind of tough to hide
Two or three different
Conflicting attitudes.

You know she never mentioned me
But she thought she might be protecting me
Or even thought she was saving me
But I never thought…
So here I am
Squared off with anger.
Intimidation would be the danger
Reputation leads to.
Everybody here is a stranger.

There is No Clear Motive

It's such a unique equation—
Try to make the worst of a situation.
Its morning again and its time to face the nation
Full of questions
About our present condition
Or if he's sure the plan doesn't need revision.
He's going to stick to his mission,
His steadfast decision.
It just seems like an obsession
Or maybe possession—
Whatever it is, its oblivious to correction
And can never be exacted with perfection
Or even attempt to claim to be any new direction.
Such is the case with our little man from Texas.

Kentucky Bourbon and the Sidewalk

This old Muddy song on the jukebox
Doesn't even come close
To drowning out any other noise
That bears a resemblance
To anything I'd recognize.

This cheap old bourbon, this spotty shot glass.
So easy to underestimate.
I tried to walk away
And let this shit wear off,
But the barstool seems to miss me when I'm gone.

The rain sounds like jackhammers on the concrete,
My heavy foot makes contact with the pavement.
I try hard, but all I get is wet.
The raindrops soak right into my skin.
The sidewalk is anther friend of mine,
It treats me the same as anyone.
I've laid down right here more than once,
But never understood the significance
That the sidewalk knows the shape I'm in.

All the Time

All your time manages to fly
Long before I even arrive
Burning your weeks, your weekends,
Like lighting cigarettes with matches in the wind,

I've often entered late at night
Long after you've turned out the lights.
Dinner's cold and left in the microwave.
So routine, happens every time I am late.

I come to bed, and its left made.
You've fallen asleep atop the spread.
I want to wake you with a kiss on your forehead,
But I just give you an extra blanket instead.

I really miss you when you're gone.
You always miss what we have done.
Every time something happens, I'm the one
To pull us out of anything gone wrong.

It seems there's so much to discuss
I wonder what's wrong with us.
Why have we grown apart so much
But I don't know if it could ever touch
The way it used to be before we had to rush.

The splendor grows sultry…inviting.
Hot like the sidewalks in July.

If I could only make it to the sunrise
And have the warmth hit my face to open my eyes.

A Panamanian jungle in my mouth
Feels like humidity…sticky like the south.

My legs are awkward as I try to amble
Separate myself from that messy linen scramble.

I manage to grumble, "it's too early in the morning."
Then crawl back under…into hiding.

Huh?

What happened to us?
We used to love each other so much.
Now, it's turned to sand
Just pouring, like water, out of my hand.
How desperate we've become
That we'd both rather be alone
Than face the challenge of loving for real.
Now it's become infinite and steel
Hard. Both our minds are made up
That it's easier to give up
Rather than fight, no matter how much it hurts.
The fact that we turn our back on what's right,
That hurts so much worse.

I have resigned
And I might just have time
To realize I might live through this
Just before I die.

I've accepted my fate,
There's nothing left to say.
Everything unknown remains
And everything used is stained.

Such as it stands, I guess that's just it.
My life never mattered, and my love is just shit.

Isn't it interesting to see the development
Or the metamorphosis between, or the accomplishment
Nearest the face of the unseen, such a lackluster involvement.

But I submit the sincerest of apologies
Just to hear you acknowledge me;
But so very much more importantly,
To know I've finally made my peace.

The saddest of the tragedies
Once again, acted so sophisticatedly,
Played out on stage so regularly
Now that it all just seems so…stationary.

Then I ask you for a remedy,
Something to make it painless for me,
But lets me have my clarity
So I can still understand what's happening.

I really must confess
I have nothing to express
I'm alone, or less.
No anxiety or duress.
It's interesting at best
Like the last thing that I've guessed.

What I don't understand is this:
Is that a nothing or a miss?
Do I favor just a little kiss?
Or just a new reason to obsess?

My favor's become a test.
The answer, locked away, like the rest
But tomorrow's just the next
Like yesterday, I need to rest.
Today is my attest
To these feelings that I get.

What I finally understood is this:
It's not morning or a miss,
But something a little more in depth
And the answer is no, not yet.

Subtle nuances, miniscule inconsistencies;
Differences between understanding and mysteries.
Like sponge seek the blissful saturation,
One yearns for something simple with duration.

A cold concoction of unidentifiable remedies.
Back door cures for the easiest of diagnoses.
One can rest upon the security Of thousands of individual hypocrisies.

My lasting impression of less influential novelties
Crossing over to some area more focused on ability.
The definition of the word, "poverty"
Relates directly to one's lack of any novelty
Or something more suited to integrity.

I can never get over that you may have loved me
And I will never comprehend why you trusted me.
But I've known for a while that you wanted the best of me.
And all the trying and waiting has gotten the rest of me.
Now, I'm left with just the memory
Of it all taken away from me.

The Night Before/The Morning After

Everything is broken
And several things are left unspoken.
The sun hides behind the horizon.

Designing a certain lackluster facade,
It seems such an innocent charade,
But built so well, that it will never fade.

I guess the more Christian of us would deduce
That time would allow for these illusions to reduce
To something more intriguing, or at least obtuse.

But the truest of those know
That no matter where we go or what we show,
Its what's left behind when we leave that shows our soul.

This is Not How its Supposed to Be

My understanding has eluded me.
My comprehension must not be
As good as I thought it was, because I see
That certain things I took for granted, I believed
Were simply incorrect…or maybe

Its so hot in here, I'm suffocating Because of the heat.
No longer contemplating, I've simply decided its time for relocating.
That, and there's nothing here worth staying for.
Everything I need has gone, so why am I delaying?
Is it fear, or is it something more complicating?
But this is not how it's supposed to be.

The lines on her face have so much depth,
Chiseled by eons of tears she's wept.
The gradual change in her elevation,
The morning sunshine, still existent in her revelation,
Even though she doesn't know the meaning of salvation.

My heart remains heavily weighted
With the swelling caused by her remaining,
Despite so many different reasons not to.
Ultimately, maybe just too used to
Being in love with this old fool.

I want to make her sure
That she never has to be insecure.
I want her to never again
Feel like she must turn to sin
Or anything else but words to express the mood she's in,

I've been saving my heart now for you
Along with every little chunk of the world I've come to
Because I think you deserve a little more
Than anything my heart alone can score,
But maybe the whole world could make you sure
Enough to always realize what's been true.
I have never stopped loving you.

Part II
Lyrics

The child, the Madman, and Me

In a darkened room,
I hear the scream of a small child
As he begins to fade.

In a darkened room,
I see the smile of a madman
As he tries to hide the pain.

In a darkened room,
I smell the blood of a rag doll
As it's torn apart.

And in this darkened room I see
That it is me,
I am all three,
The child, the madman and me.

Porchlight

Step outside
Leave the porch light on
Take a walk with me
Out to the dawn
Creep away from everything
Everything gone wrong
But leave the porch light on.
So I can find my way back home

    I carry home my trouble
    I can't see
    In the darkness
    Leave the porch light on
    Leave the porch light on

It's foggy outside
And the wind is cold
And bitter against my back as I go
But I can't come back
Back home alone
You didn't leave the porch light on
I can't find my way back home

    I have trouble
    Seeing in the dark
    I struggle
    To stay warm in the cold

Leave the porch light on
Leave the porch light on

Not that I compare myself to Jesus
Nor that I like listening to preachers
Or know anything about
What they have to teach us

They ask me,
Hey,
What do you live for?

I say,
Hey man,
Its something you don't know.
It's the thing that hides
In the back of your mind
Where demons ride
On the threads of your time.

They ask me,
Hey,
Can I have a slice of your life?
I say,
Hey man,
Get in line.

Because everyone wants to watch me
Crash and burn,
But no one cares to listen
To what I have learned.

Crutch

I'm not your stepping stone
I'm not your scapegoat
I'm not who you can run to
When you can't escape, no.

(I'm your crutch)
You wear me like a crown
(Gave you too much)
Use your smallest finger to hold me down

You singled me out
Now I'm without
And I can't fall for you anymore.
You broke my castle down
Now my heart is exposed
The walls came down around me
Now I'm left in the cold.

(I'm your crutch)
But you're dragging me down
(It's not good enough)
To carry the weight of your frown
But you turned your back
And I slipped through the cracks
And now I can't fall any lower.

Used To Be.

I used to be perfect
Everything was a sure fit
I didn't know what to do with it.
Now, it seems I've lost it.

You could've had something
It could've been worth it.

I was young once
Such a silly nuance
But what's the use?
I fell for your worthwhile
You wanted my innocent smile
But I've wasted all my innocence on youth

And now I'm a little older
And time has gotten somewhat bolder
What's so good about having youth?
It's cold when I sleep alone
And I know you aren't coming home
How could I have been such a fool?

Now all I've got is nothing
All I have is worthless.

Window on the World

You shake your finger to me in disgust,
But it is I who should mistrust
Yesterday is only a memory
Tomorrow's just a dream to me.

Down the hall, up the stairs near the bathroom
Trying to poke a hole in the side of a vacuum
I see life through the eyes of a bedroom window
Saturday morning's a little left of innuendo.

It's been sixteen years
Since I've been here
Nothing's what it seems
Kind of like a cloudy dream
And dreams are almost everything

It took a while to open you
To find nothing when I broke through
I left you broken on the floor
You'll never engulf me anymore
You bled away your sins toward me
But, just like you, I am empty

I walked down the hall, up the stairs to the bathroom
For the last time. I took one last look at the vacuum
It blew away like ashes in the wind
No more bedroom daydreams again.

When I lied, you saw right through me
When you cried, your tears consumed me
When you tried, I heard, "abuse me"
And when you died, your blood consumed me.

I saw the serenity in your eyes
And I knew I'd call them home.
But it hurt so much when I couldn't find
The same peace inside my own
Now you're left with only virtue
And I am left with pride
I didn't think I could ever hurt you
Every time you cried.

When you looked, you saw right through me
When I took, you gave right to me
When I spoke, you heard, "you soothe me"
But when you checked, you never knew me.

These gray walls remind me softly
Of what I now call home
And of the security it cot me
Now I'm all alone
Now I'm left with only memories
And you are left with less
They remind me what a fool I'd been
And how much I've made a mess.

When you looked you saw into me
Saw the monster that consumed me
Still you stood there right beside me
Even though you had to fight me

Now you're part of my nightmares
And I can never sleep alone
Something hallowed left me there
And I'll never find my home
I took the calmness from your eyes
That I could never find in mine
I left you there with my disguise
And ran away to escape my crime.

Now it's on my hands
It will never wash away
Now it's on my hands
They'll be forever stained.

Tomorrow's like eternity
Another day without you
Yesterday I wish I could see
That life is barren without you
All this time's gone by, I've missed you
A few more hours and I'll be with you
I'm sorry that I left you crying
I didn't understand that you were dying
At my hands!

When I looked I saw inside me
Now I found what I've been missing
When I heard, it was so frightening
But I couldn't help but listen.
The morning's cold and I've been thinking
As I hang here from these gallows
From now on everything's sinking
Into dust, my body's hollow.

I've gone to the one place I've always wanted
And now I'm not alone
When I see you, I am haunted
I've finally found my home.

When   I turned, I found you beside me
When   I felt, you were inside me
When   I left, I felt you guide me
When   I knelt, You did accept me.

Torment

I was never one to back down from a challenge
Even though the decision I'm left with
No matter what, is slightly less than worth it.
You always seem to deem me as perfect
And, though I'm a recipe for disaster,
I've asked often if I really matter
And what's the use
If I remember right, it's never been the truth

I try so hard to be everything you need
But I end up so far from the one thing you se
A small taste of shallow inconsistency
Or a real awakening that you finally see through me
I'm not what you thought, or at least don't appear to be
But you're left with a start, "that's all I ever could be"

Yesterday's a new day, and I'm listless again
I beg for a few days to get back, to begin
With what I had just a short time ago
A simple understanding, and the fact that I know
That at least I can be happy, even though I am alone

But torment is a motherfucker, a killer of souls.
It can leave even the strongest warrior broken
With nothing but guilt, or some other token
That everything he's known and believed
Has been nothing more than innocent stupidity
And the last thing on my mind As my head hit's the floor—
How will I find
The ability to be everything she's looking for?

I guess I'll never know Because now I've decided that tomorrow
Will never come, Because I'm always better off
The way I should have been from kickoff…
Alone

The torment pushes through,
Like the fading of youth
And leaves me with the welcome solitude
Because I know I will never amount to
Anything that they wanted me to.

Sunshine and Possibility Given to Immobility

She holds her cigarette like a man
Not near the tips of her fingers
But near the palm of her hand.

It's late at night and her guests have gone
Now she's faced with the sudden harshness
That she's in this big place alone

She faces the mirror of premonition
Kind of like a lover in solemn repose
The tingle in her is more than just intuition

She's just finished hanging pictures with no frames
But it's just as well for her because
All the people in the photos have no names.

That seems to be the telling of her tale
A story of over simplified anonymity
Where every page is blank and rather pale.

But tomorrow's a different day,
Full of sunshine and possibilities,
But she'll spend it in bed, same as she did yesterday.

Beco

He lost his battle with the sun;
His demons in disease had finally won,
But he felt no pain, like he went to sleep.
Like he tried so hard, but couldn't keep
Up. Life is just so fast, so far ahead
That it doesn't notice when one of us is dead,
But we did.

Our times together, I thought would be forever.
Bravery never came into question;
All those memories blend together.

Five weeks seem like an eternity.
Just like all twenty million memories
In a rainstorm developing into a hurricane,
A flat line can make a heart race.
A silent prayer in the middle of the night;
A last ditch effort to beg for a life.
Everything went quiet.